CRICKET MASALA

CRICKET MASALA

MARK RAY

ABC
BOOKS

Published by ABC Books for the
AUSTRALIAN BROADCASTING CORPORATION
GPO Box 9994 Sydney NSW 2001

First published October 2002

National Library of Australia
Cataloguing-in-Publication entry
Ray, Mark
    Cricket masala.

    ISBN 0 7333 1093 1

    1. Cricket players - Australia - Pictorial works.
    2. Cricket - Australia - Pictorial works. I. Australian Broadcasting
Corporation. II. Title.

796.3580922

Design Graham Rendoth / Reno Design, Sydney R21096
Typesetting Reno Design, in Trajan and Joanna
Scanning PageSet, Melbourne
Printing Printed and bound by KHL, Singapore, for Imago

5 4 3 2 1

For Margaret, Elizabeth, Simon, Hannah and Lucy

CONTENTS

Acknowledgments

Many people helped me to compile this collection. The Australian team and its staff were always accessible and co-operative. I'd like to thank all the players, especially Mark Taylor, Steve Waugh, Shane Warne, Adam Gilchrist, Justin Langer and Matthew Hayden. Of the support staff, manager Steve Bernard, his assistant Mike Walsh and physiotherapist Errol Alcott were always helpful, while the amazingly affable media manager, Brian Murgatroyd, was outstanding.

Many Australian journalists toured with me from 1995 to 2002 and all have held my tape recorder or my laptop while I tried to get a picture. In particular, I must thank Malcolm Conn for his company on two brilliant excursions: the road trip from Islamabad to Peshawar in November 1998 and the train trip from Colombo to Kandy for the Esala Perehera in August 1999. ABC Radio's Glenn Mitchell and AAP's Steve Larkin accompanied me on many walks in Sri Lanka in '99 as did News Ltd photographer Phil Hillyard in India in 2001. Mike Horan, Martin Blake, John Townsend, Malcolm Knox, Mark Fuller, Peter Hanlon, Robert Craddock, Will Swanton, Ron Reed, Jim Tucker, Peter Roebuck, Mike Coward, Jim Maxwell, Tim Lane, Peter Walsh, Cole Hitchcock, Michael Donaldson and Michael Crutcher all provided good company, some in tough times.

Cricket is blessed with many fine photographers, many of whom have encouraged my amateur dabbling. I'd like to mention Graham and Diana Morris from London, Brett Costello, Hamish Blair, David White, Shaun Botterill, Ben Radford, Trent Parke, Jack Atley, William West, Dave Gray, Patrick Eagar and Mueen ud din Hameed.

In England I also received support from journalists Michael Henderson, David Hopps, Rob Steen, Peter Deeley, Simon Briggs, and Tim De Lisle, Matthew Engel, Steven Lynch and everyone else at Wisden. I must also thank Sir Paul Getty for his hospitality in 1997 and Colin Ingleby-McKenzie for allowing me to photograph him in the Long Room at Lord's. In India, support and advice came from Clayton Murzello, Darshak Mehta, Harsha Bhogle, Gulu Ezekiel, Nandu and Usha Bhende, Rahul and Vidhu Bhagat. In Pakistan, from Fareshteh Gati-Aslam, Shahid Hussain and Bashir Khan. In Sri Lanka, from Rohan Wijeyaratna.

I'd also like to make special mention of Swan Richards and everyone at the Crusaders in Melbourne for their generous assistance and excellent company in England in 1997; and Barry Knight, Yogam Devendran and Sri Lankan Airlines for my second visit to the island in April 2000.

I must also thank Stuart Neal, Brigitta Doyle, Lindsay Somerville and the staff at ABC Enterprises for their excellent work in the production of this book.

Finally I thank all the people I met and photographed on the road in those seven years.

Prints of these and other photographs by Mark Ray can be purchased at www.markray.net

Dennis Lillee and Jeff Thomson conducting a fast-bowling clinic — Lord's, June 1997

RAW
POWER!
Daily Telegraph
fast bowler '97
RAW
POWER!
Daily Telegraph
fast bowler '97

AUSTRALIA

1995–2002

After the swarming passions of the subcontinent and the often shabby hotch-potch that is English cricket, the Australian game can seem ultra modern and ruthlessly efficient. At most levels the play is aggressive and well planned. The infrastructure is sound. There is a commitment to excellence that is foreign to the English. Factional politics play a much smaller role in Australia than in other countries. The major grounds are spotless structures of steel and concrete that gleam under the antipodean sun. It is no surprise that touring teams enjoy playing here.

For me, touring in various capacities every summer for eighteen years became a chore. The dream job for every cricket-loving boy can pale with repetition. Even the most successful players lose their edge towards the end of their careers, wilting under the pressure. But while the enthusiasm is there, there is much to be enjoyed — especially the superb facilities which allow the best players to display their skills to the full. The distances between venues, the flights they necessitate and the small number of tour games against the states mean there is little time to see things outside the major venues. Occasionally, visiting journalists, under more accommodating deadlines, find the time to do a drive, often along the coast from Melbourne to Adelaide. A few have taken the train across the Nullarbor Plain to Perth. For local journalists, work demands and the need always to be with the Australian team mean life is a series of airports, planes, hotels and press boxes.

The French street photographer Henri Cartier-Bresson once said that the place he found hardest to photograph was his own country. It was so familiar that it was difficult to see it with the fresh eyes that make the best pictures. Certainly, trying to snap pictures while working with a laptop on the Australian cricket circuit had its limitations. Visiting a foreign country gives you those fresh eyes, the spark you need on long tours.

Baggy green cap — third Test v West Indies, Adelaide, December 2000

With conditions so congenial and memories for past players so good, an Australian summer attracts retired cricketers from all over the world. The English love coming to Australia to watch cricket because of the long history of the Ashes and the close, if occasionally testy, relationship this has produced. We go back a long way, in cricket as in many things. An Australian summer offers warm and usually dry weather, quality cricket and good company. Although the weather varies and the quality of the cricket has been sadly below par in the recent past, England offers the same hospitality to Australians who visit during an Ashes tour. But there are differences. Some English people see Australians as overly aggressive, a little too ruthless. Australians see that attitude as a thinly disguised excuse for English inadequacies, a ready acceptance of second-best. As a boy I saw Fred Trueman at the SCG. He had the crowd in his hand, chatting and sipping a beer while fielding on the fence. He was loved in Australia as a forthright, tough, talented and charismatic English cricketer. Australian crowds see Darren Gough in a similar way, though he's not in Trueman's class as a bowler. David Gower is different, the archetypical elegant English gentleman player. But Gower was no arrogant upper-class Pom. He was admired in Australia because he was a beautiful player and a witty, unpretentious bloke.

West Indians love touring Australia. They have to pinch themselves when they see our hard, fast and bouncy pitches which suit both their great fast bowlers and their gifted, attacking batsmen. And they know they will be in a passionate contest with Australian teams. At least that was the case during their dominance of world cricket from the mid-'80s to the mid-'90s. Players from that era — Michael Holding or Viv Richards — have visited Australia recently and have been aghast at the insipid cricket played by their successors. Australia can be a merciless venue if you are not up to the challenge.

One of the strengths of Australian cricket is what is often called the peer group influence. Mark Taylor and Steve Waugh were very much their own men and did not rely that much on advice from previous captains. They didn't have to. Both inherited, without thinking about it, the Australian tradition of attacking cricket, of taking risks to win matches, of employing imaginative tactics. The greatly increased number of results in Test matches around the world owes much to the influence of these two men and the traditions to which they belong. But behind all the prominent contemporary names are the greats of the past — Richie Benaud, the Chappells, Dennis Lillee — who in various ways are available to pass on knowledge and, even more importantly, attitude. That they are involved, whether professionally or informally, adds to the richness of the Australian scene. Ricky Ponting, who will be another great Australian captain, will honour that tradition.

The failing for which Australian cricket has been widely criticised has been sledging. It is often unnecessary, pointless and immature, but it is hardly as damaging to the international game as critics argue. In the 2002 series in South Africa, local broadcasters turned up the volume on the stump microphones, allowing the critics to discover the general inanity of the so-called sledging. I've always been happier to forgive a team a little sledging if it helps them play with passion. Far worse to see cricket teams playing meekly, not doing justice to themselves or the game. But it is a matter of circumstances. A little sledging can improve a Test match. It has no place in the under-14s. Sadly, the rapacious eye of the television camera has highlighted the behaviour of the big names and so encouraged park cricketers to think they must sledge to be competitive.

The international cricket circuit is nothing if not varied. Muslims, Hindus, Parsees, Buddhists, Rastafarians, Christians, atheists and agnostics, arch conservatives and Marxist subversives, rich and poor — they're all in there, playing, administering and following the game in unique ways. Compared with the more exotic varieties, the Australian game might appear colourless, but it is inspired by as much passion as any of the others.

⁓

Shane Warne making a cheese sandwich after play — third Test v West Indies, Melbourne, December 1996

Dennis Lillee coaching at the cricket academy – Adelaide, August 1996

Bob Hawke launching a cricket book – first Test v Pakistan, Brisbane, November 1999

Adam Gilchrist — Prime Minister's XI v West Indies, Canberra, December 2000

Mark Taylor at the height of the players' dispute — end of the second Test v New Zealand, Perth, November 1997

Ricky Ponting — Sydney, February 1998

Justin Langer and his daughter — Perth Airport, November 2000

Matthew Hayden — team camp, Mooloolaba, Queensland, October 1999

Brett Lee at practice – Brisbane, November 2000

Jason Gillespie watching replays — end of the second Test v West Indies, Perth, December 2000

Darrell Hair — end of the fifth Test v West Indies, Sydney, January 2001

Paul Kelly behind the bowler's arm – third Test v West Indies, Melbourne, December 1996

Courtney Walsh at the end of his last match in Australia – fifth Test, Sydney, January 2001

Brian Lara at practice – before the first Test, Brisbane, November 1996

Bradman Pavilion – third Test v West Indies, Adelaide, December 2000

Jimmy Adams at practice — before the fourth Test, Adelaide, January 1997

WACA scoreboard — fifth Test v West Indies, Perth, February 1997

Michael Holding – fifth Test v West Indies, Perth, February 1997

Stuart MacGill — third Test v South Africa, Sydney, January 2002

The Hill — NSW v New Zealand, Newcastle, November 1997

Cousins on Christmas holidays — Taree, NSW, January 2002

Young girl — Northern Territory XI v West Indies, Alice Springs, November 2000

ENGLAND

1997, 2001

The crowds in India can get to you after a while. There are just so many people, most with a natural compulsion to congregate in doorways, on footpaths and staircases — any place where people need room to pass. In England the claustrophobia that can affect Australians is cultural rather than physical. The weight of English history hangs over everything, especially a conservative game like cricket. It stifles reform and encourages the acceptance of low standards. 'Still, mustn't grumble,' as comedian Alexei Sayle advises venomously.

This attitude has left the English game marooned in mediocrity ever since Allan Border's 1989 Australians regained the Ashes. In the ensuing thirteen years, Australia has consistently set new standards, on and off the field, while England has muddled along. Too many people in English cricket cannot break free of the past, the years of glory, to admit they have been wrong and make the necessary corrections.

Writing in the *Guardian* after the death of the Queen Mother in April 2002, Hugo Young discussed the furore that erupted when a BBC newsreader did not wear a black tie when announcing the passing of a royal born at the start of the previous century. Young compared the old world and the new. 'But for most Americans, the past gets in the way of the future. They look backwards as much in apprehension as celebration … history does not infuse everything they do. Respect for history is not a precondition of contemporary action. The past does not suck them in, preoccupy them, define their sense of self.'

Young turned to his homeland. 'Here the national psyche is inextricably defined by the past, the period of national greatness that has gone. For some people, clinging to the past is a way of remembering that life undoubtedly was

Rock band — Stonehenge, July 1997

better however many decades ago. The past and its icons seem to supply the strategies by which we stoically remind ourselves that things, alas, can never be the same again.'

Young did wonder whether all Britons succumbed to 'this wallowing in the past, this old British disease' which has been 'the enemy of the future'. After all, this is the nation of Ian Botham, the Sex Pistols, film-maker Ken Loach and the irreverent spirit that animates the north. For every obsessed middle-aged autograph collector, there is an energetic Barmy Army backpacker. And while county cricket reluctantly staggers into the twentieth century, someone somehow managed to overcome the national inertia and turn a disused London power station on the Thames into the wonderful Tate Modern. Maybe those responsible for that art gallery should be seconded onto the England and Wales Cricket Board without delay.

Writing in the 2002 *Wisden Cricketers' Almanack*, editor Graeme Wright described county cricket as 'a confederacy of mediocrity'. But is anyone listening? Many people in English cricket rail against that mediocrity. Crowds at Test matches boo inept play by their own team. In the north especially, pretensions are pricked by humour, shortcomings derided by self-deprecating wit. Apart from the 'flying gherkin', that bizarre media centre at Lord's, recent renovations at the grand old ground have managed successfully to combine the modern with the best of the old. Hampshire County Cricket Club should be commended for building an excellent modern ground outside Southampton. Yet at Taunton in Somerset, the Ian Botham Stand is a red-brick monstrosity built at an angle to the boundary. This was due to the lack of space between the ground and the river but no one bothered to find out how to ensure that the seats in the stand faced the field. Spectators have to sit at a slight angle to the play. As well, the stand is always partly empty as the sightscreens are set in front of it. It's a depressing shemozzle, typical of the attitude that asks 'Why do something properly when you can half do it?'.

That 'English disease' Young described infuriates many Australians who see England's long history as something of a curse and suffer cultural claustrophobia under its weight. Other Australians love it because it is so different from our brief, 'white' history.

Ashes tours traditionally start with the ritual of mutual psychoanalysis. As the Australians arrive at Heathrow, the English start asking why we are so competitive, why winning is so important to us. The Australians ask why England always accepts mediocrity, why it's so blind to its shortcomings. But all this is done over a foundation of historical closeness. Perhaps it's sibling rivalry writ large.

Touring England can still be a great deal of fun. The English are generally excellent company, with a celebrated sense of humour that sits well with Australians. And English pubs are brilliant. During an Ashes tour, the evening trips on the motorways after a day's play can be awfully boring and the hotels you arrive at can be infuriating — poorly run and shoddily appointed. England is still notorious for its poor service. The one country in the cricket world where I've had trouble with the heat is England. When the summer warms up, the airconditioning in many hotels breaks down, if it exists at all. Rooms quickly come to resemble saunas and tempers unravel. Yet England also offers so much. One night in London you can see a great rock band at an excellent venue, the next Alfred Brendel playing Schubert at the Festival Hall. One minute you can be standing in front of a Turner at the Tate and half an hour later downing a pint in a wonderful little pub in Soho. The drabness of some of the cities can get you down, but if you have time to avoid the motorways, you can pass through hundreds of wonderful English cities, towns and villages. You might be in the rolling mystical hills around Stonehenge, the chocolate-box world of the Cotswolds, the austere Yorkshire Moors or the imposing Lake District.

All this is brilliant stuff. And, despite that infuriating English obsession with the past, even the most irreverent colonial cricket lover will be moved by his or her first sight of Lord's.

Scoreboard — third Test, Manchester, July 1997

Social match – private ground, Northamptonshire, July 1997

Homeless and unemployed men queueing for work as cleaners after the day's play — second Test, Lord's, June 1997

Colin Ingleby-McKenzie, then MCC president – Long Room, Lord's, June 1997

England captain Michael Atherton — before the third Test, Manchester, July 1997

Dennis Lillee and Jeff Thomson conducting a fast-bowling clinic — Lord's, June 1997

Omitted batsman Michael Slater after practice – before the third Test, Manchester, July 1997

Glenn McGrath at a press conference after taking 8 for 38 – second Test, Lord's, June 1997

Glenn McGrath and Ian Healy applauding Steve Waugh's second century of the third Test – Manchester, July 1997

Keith Miller at Sir Paul Getty's ground — Wormsley, July 1997

Sir Paul Getty at his ground — Wormsley, July 1997

David Gower, Mark Taylor and Glenn McGrath — end of the second Test, Lord's, June 1997

Autograph collector – practice day before the third Test, Manchester, July 1997

England captain Nasser Hussain – practice day before the fourth Test, Leeds, August 2001

Shoaib Akhtar outside the Australian team hotel – Kensington Gardens, London, August 2001

Jason Gillespie — New Road, Worcester, June 2001

Press box — Hove, Sussex, August 2001

Alec Stewart – fourth Test, Leeds, August 2001

Pakistani youth bowling in a street game – Hyde Park, Leeds, August 2001

Practice session — Keswick, Lake District, June 2001

Souvenir cricket balls —
Portobello Road Market,
London, August 2001

Gladiator — fourth Test, Leeds, August 2001

Marxist historian and author Mike Marqusee – outside Lord's, second Test, June 1997

Spectators at a tour game — New Road, Worcester, June 2001

Tour match — Taunton, July 2001

INDIA

1997, 2001

Our taxi resembled an ambulance. We were halfway through the third Test of a dramatic, high-quality series and the tour was starting to take its toll. Chennai was hot and humid. After five weeks working hard in India, the nine-hour days in a stifling open-air press box were melting our remaining resistance. Of the four Australian journalists, one was on antibiotics for a persistent ear infection, one was suffering diarrhoea and nausea, another had a bad dose of hotel 'flu, and I had just finished a course of antibiotics for a stomach infection and was beginning to go weak at the knees with heat exhaustion.

As we drove back to our hotel after a day's play, my colleague in the front seat tried to raise our spirits. 'Hey guys, there's a great photo — that bird sitting on that bloke's head.' He pointed to a large statue on the wide expanse of beach that followed the edge of the busy road. 'That's no bloke,' I said. 'That's Mahatma Gandhi.' Every village in India boasts a statue of Gandhi, the beloved father of the nation.

Most journalists criticise touring Australian cricketers for their reluctance to embrace the local cultures, but some journalists are just as guilty of that neglect. Recent Australian teams have tried harder to open their minds to places like India, but it is not easy. They travel, play or train every day and security concerns mean local officials react by surrounding visiting teams with heavy protection. And even when some adventurous players sneak out from under the security blanket, they are quickly recognised by dozens, then hundreds, of fans and a quiet walk turns into a noisy traffic jam. Often it's just easier to stay in the hotel.

The first time I went to Mumbai, a four-day stopover on the way back from England in August 1997, I came across the Azad Maidan, one of the two large dusty parks in the centre of the city where cricket games are played during

Boy paying homage to Mahatma Gandhi — Visakhapatnam, April 2001

64

every daylight hour. It was mid-afternoon, school was out and boys were playing everywhere. I stopped near one game and as soon as they saw me these boys ran over. I told them I'd talk to them and maybe give them something if they went back to their game and let me take some photos. Finally they returned to their pitch. The first time a batsman was hit on the pads they did not appeal to their own umpire but swung around and appealed as one to me, stationed at deep cover. Fortunately, I had the camera to my eyes. I had taken some spare prints of famous cricketers with me and later handed them out to the boys. After that I wandered over to a row of sheds that ran along the edge of the maidan. Within seconds I was inside the Young Zorastrians Cricket Club, sipping a cool drink and meeting the elderly members who were playing cards over glasses of whiskey or gin. One of them had umpired the Australians in a Test match in the 1960s. 'I hope they behaved themselves,' I said. 'Oh yes,' Mr Mamsa said. 'They were all very fine gentlemen. Mr Ian Chappell, a very fine man.' In 2001 I went back to the clubrooms with a pile of photos I shot in '97 and was treated as an old friend.

While the maidans show Indian cricket at the grassroots, the major grounds display the nation's near-manic passion for the international game and its superstars. As Indian journalists told us, the passion is not necessarily deep. It is more like the passion for movie stars. It is fame more than great skill that fires the frenzy. Mumbai's Brabourne Stadium was a Test ground until the 1970s, when political infighting saw Wankhede Stadium take the major role. Brabourne had acted both as venue and hotel for touring teams, with accommodation in the rooms run by the owners, the exclusive Cricket Club of India (CCI). The 2001 Australian team played Mumbai at Brabourne, with every run applauded by hundreds of excited schoolchildren. After play, the elderly members of CCI took over, turning the place into a genteel living museum of the British Raj — without the British.

Wankhede's crowd was incredibly warm, giving the Australians a wonderful reception when they won the first Test in three days. On the second morning, the streets outside the ground were jam-packed as thousands jostled for tickets. 'This is Sachin's queue,' a man said to me. The national hero, master batsman Sachin Tendulkar, had been not out overnight, guaranteeing a full house of 50,000 that day. As the crowd inside roared his every run, those in the queues outside became more impatient to reach those tiny holes in the wall where the priceless tickets were dispensed.

Chennai's Chepauk ground was the noisiest of the three Test venues we visited. For five tense days, capacity crowds of 60,000 kept up a roar that combined with the stifling heat to make this third Test an exhausting experience. Kolkata's Eden Gardens is one of the great cricket grounds of the world, the Melbourne Cricket Ground on ecstasy. It can hold up to 100,000 and police security is strict. (I needed four passes just to leave and return to the press box after a visit to the scoreboard area on the other side.) Each morning tens of thousands of fans would form long, circular queues all over the dusty maidan outside the stadium. Occasionally they would burst into cheers as a mischievous taxi driver would break ranks, leave the huge traffic jam and cut across the maidan, and its queues, to get his passenger closer to the gates. When each person in the queue reached the end, he or she was confronted by a low, tiny hole in a paling fence where cash and ticket were awkwardly exchanged. Then there was the race across to the designated gate and entry into the magnificent arena.

Away from those great grounds, India's laneways offer a quieter, more intimate world, a place where you can meet and talk with people without being submerged by huge crowds. Kids will follow you, but you can shoo them away long enough to chat to families who sit outside their houses and welcome western visitors with the warmth and charm typical of the subcontinent. And down every laneway, you'll see someone swinging a cricket bat.

—

Boy on a beach — Visakhaptnam, April 2001

Bowler on a maidan — Pune, March 2001

Sachin Tendulkar and Shane Warne – before the start of the first Test, Wankhede Stadium, Mumbai, February 2001

Girl selling newspapers – Mumbai, February 2001

A minute's silence for Sir Donald Bradman – before the start of the first Test, Mumbai, February 2001

Shane Warne thanking the crowd — end of the first Test, Mumbai, February 2001

Harbhajan Singh at practice — before One-Day International, Indore, March 2001

Schoolgirls – Australia v Mumbai, Brabourne Stadium, Mumbai, February 2001

After play — Cricket Club of India, Australia v Mumbai, Brabourne Stadium, Mumbai, February 2001

Boy in a ticket queue – first Test, Mumbai, February 2001

Ticket queue – first Test, Mumbai, February 2001

A tailor and his family — Mumbai, February 2001

Sourav Ganguly, Sachin Tendulkar and Javagal Srinath on a poster — Kajuri Bazaar, Indore, March 2001

Schoolboys — Azad Maidan, Mumbai, August 1997

Maidan games — Mumbai, February 2001

Young Zorastrians Cricket Club – Azad Maidan, Mumbai, August 1997

Parsee Cyclists Cricket Club – Azad Maidan, Mumbai, August 1997

Near Azad Maidan, Mumbai, August 1997

Harishchandra Shivalkar, 60-year-old off spinner — Azad Maidan, February 2001

Policeman with confiscated posters – One-Day International, Indore, March 2001

THE FOUNDATION STONE
OF
NIVEDITA BHAVAN
(UDAYAN GIRLS WING)
WAS LAID BY
STEVE WAUGH
AUSTRALIAN CRICKET CAPTAIN
AND
PATRON, UDAYAN
ON
JULY 21ST 1998

Student — Udayan home for children of lepers, Kolkata, March 2001

Bat on a rock — Visakhaptnam, April 2001

Laneway – Visakhaptnam, April 2001

Batmaker's roadside stall — Nagpur, February 2001

Parents buying their son a new bat at a roadside stall — Nagpur, February 2001

Two-minute net operation after play — second Test, Kolkata, March 2001

VVS Laxman's and Rahul Dravid's gear after play – second Test, Kolkata, March 2001

Ticket windows — second Test, Kolkata, March 2001

Man buying a ticket — second Test, Kolkata, March 2001

Ticket queue – second Test, Kolkata, March 2001

SRI LANKA

1999, 2000

After sipping Lion lagers at a terrace bar of the old colonial Galle Face Hotel on our third or fourth evening in Colombo and watching a solar eclipse sink gently into the Indian Ocean, we knew the 1999 tour of Sri Lanka would be special. The sight of a glowing sliver of sun falling quietly through the horizon was always going to be hard to beat, and so it proved. Although the edges of the monsoon season ruined two of the three Test matches, the travelling press rated this tour the best they had covered. An evening drink on that terrace bar, with the ocean in front of us, became a ritual after a hot and sweaty day's work. We saw dozens of beautiful sunsets and, appropriately, Glenn Mitchell of ABC Radio ended his professionally self-narrated home video of the tour with a long, silent shot of the final sunset.

The Australian team and its support staff were somewhat hamstrung by security concerns on this tour. When it was over we learned that there had been seventy-five security personnel in and around the hotel we stayed in across the road from Galle Face Green. And while most members of the team played it safe and stayed within the hotel, the journalists roamed free and easy throughout Colombo. Still, the Green offered plenty of entertainment for those whose social life revolved around their room's balcony. The 'beach' next to the Green is narrow and rough so most visitors come to watch, to walk or to play cricket rather than to swim. Busloads of visitors to the capital, Sri Lankans as well as foreigners, stop at the Green to watch the crowds or simply stare out to sea. This is a regular excursion for schoolchildren, always immaculate in their white uniforms. If these visitors are lucky they might see a spectacular monsoon storm approaching the city from the Indian Ocean to the south-west of the island. On weekends, there might be thirty or forty games of pick-up cricket going on along the dusty expanse. (Despite the best intentions of a local postcard which has been doctored to show the area as vividly grassed, the 'Green'

Schoolgirls – Galle Face Green, Colombo, September 1999

of the title derives more from hope than fact.) On Sundays, young courting couples observe their own ritual, promenading along the concrete pathway between the cricket games and the sea under the privacy of umbrellas.

Most international cricket tours involve tiring internal flights. Only England and Sri Lanka can be done on the road. However, in Sri Lanka there are no long, deadening motorway journeys every few days. Admittedly, some of the road trips in Sri Lanka were frightening. Sri Lankans have little road sense. Galle Road is the closest the island has to a highway and runs south along the coast from Colombo. It is one lane each way, with buildings encroaching on its rough edges. Tuk-tuks, cyclists and pedestrians hold to the sides while cars and buses treat the middle of the road like a racetrack. One night we sat on the balcony of a restaurant on Galle Road at Hikkaduwa, a backpacker beach resort just north of Galle, and watched as one bus passed another which was already passing the slowest of the three in the middle of the main drag. All this only a few feet from the building we were in. One error and down comes the balcony. This was hilarious as well as frightening, a typical combination on the subcontinent.

Sri Lanka was once known as Serendib and in 1999 there was a fair amount of serendipity about our tour. That black cloud of civil war that hovered over the island never affected us. Things just seemed to work out for the best. For the second Test in Galle we booked, confirmed and re-confirmed our hotel rooms yet were denied them on the day, a party of German tourists given preference because they were a source of regular income. We ended up back in Hikkaduwa. We had been warned that the town was a little seedy, but it had been cleaned up in the months before we arrived, with one foreign bar owner imprisoned for drug offences. We were there outside tourist season and life was delightful. The afternoon we arrived a colleague and I went for a walk along the beach and met Sugath, a barefoot, ponytailed guy in his mid-twenties. He asked us if we wanted to take a boat out to see the reef. We declined but I kept up a conversation. That evening I met him and Upul, his best friend, at one of the bars that run down to the beach. A few days later some of us visited the village in the jungle where Sugath and Upul lived. It was a beautiful town of some 150 houses scattered through the lush bushland. We spent that night drinking beer in the one-room mud-brick hut the two had built at the back of Upul's sister's house.

Sugath and Upul were not as passionate about cricket as most Sri Lankans, but when I returned six months later there was a family game going on behind the hut. Upul's brother is the laughing batsman on page 116.

Sri Lankans, like others on the subcontinent, are warm and friendly hosts, always delighted that you have come to visit their country. In Colombo we also met members of the lively and friendly expat community with whom some of us have maintained contact. As one Yorkshire-born schoolteacher said, 'I love it here. We have too many rules in the west.' It might be safer and more organised in the west because of those rules, but it's not as much fun. You can't eat a great, cheap meal, walk outside, immediately pile into three tuk-tuks and offer the driver who gets back to the hotel first a big tip. Nor can you do a favour for a young soldier who has just stopped your tuk-tuk at a security roadblock and asked your driver to deliver a bottle of arrack, the local spirit made from coconuts, to his mate at the next roadblock. And although many Sri Lankans are too poor to go to restaurants, none starve because the island is rich in fruit, nuts and fish. Any time you want a drink you only have to cut a hole in a coconut. Perhaps that is why Sri Lankans smile so much.

When news around the world and at home has been appalling, there has been one welcome development: the Tamil Tigers and the new government have laid down arms and, for the first time in twenty years, are seriously talking peace.

—

End of practice – Stella Maris College, Negombo, September 1999

Steve Waugh after the toss — first Test, Kandy, September 1999

Under the scoreboard — first Test, Kandy, September 1999

Acting captain Shane Warne after Australia lost the first Test — Kandy, September 1999

First Test — Kandy, September 1999

First Test — Kandy, September 1999

Street game – Kandy, September 1999

Street game – Kandy, September 1999

Shane Warne during a tour match — Colombo, September 1999

Buddhist monks watching a One-Day International — Galle Fort, August 1999

Doug Walters during a club tour match — Colombo, April 2000

Courting couple — Galle Face Green, Colombo, September 1999

Scoreboard at a tour match – Colombo, September 1999

Spectator at a tour match — Colombo, September 1999

Village game – near Hikkaduwa, April 2000

Laneway — Slave Island, Colombo, September 1999

Beach — Hikkaduwa, September 1999

Fishing boat – Negombo, September 1999

Family — Negombo, September 1999

Children's game – Negombo, September 1999

PAKISTAN

1998

Every morning outside the courtroom of Justice Malik Mohammed Qayuum's hearing into match-fixing at the Lahore High Court, there was a tall, balding man in his forties. Like many people on the subcontinent, he seemed to pass the time just standing around and, like most men in Pakistan, he carried himself with quiet dignity, elegant in cream shalwar qamiz, the loose, flowing national costume of large shirt and light trousers. He knew I was a western journalist covering the inquiry and happily exchanged good mornings with me. Eventually I asked him what brought him to the court each day. He glanced around, leant over and quietly told me he was head of security. A year earlier there had been a bombing in the grounds of the beautiful, pink-brick complex that houses the province's High Court. It was a volatile place.

When we were there for the inquiry the other major case was the lengthy saga of corruption charges against Asif Ali Zardari, the husband of exiled former prime minister Benazir Bhutto. Whenever he was let out of prison to attend another hearing, armed police and soldiers swarmed the streets outside the court complex. Political infighting and attendant violence were either simmering away below the surface or openly interrupting daily life. In Pakistan, I always had the impression things were not as they seemed, like the camera shop in Lahore that doubled as an illegal cricket betting shop. And in the midst of all this were warm, friendly, impressive men ready to welcome westerners showing interest in their nation.

I use the word 'men' because most women in Pakistan are hidden away, either behind veils, behind the front doors of their homes or behind a code of defensive conduct. Only in the cosmopolitan cities, Karachi and Lahore, do women show their hair and faces and, occasionally, wear western clothes. The treatment of women, however much

Tea stall – Darra, North-West Frontier Province, November 1998

a part of the culture, tends after a while to depress the most sympathetic westerner. Yet as with most things in Pakistan there is another side to the issue, something that undermines first impressions. For example, in 1998 Pakistan had more women cricket writers than either England or Australia, and they were tough, confident, campaigning journalists. Also, it is worth recalling that in December 1988 Benazir Bhutto became the first elected woman leader in the Muslim world.

The best aspect of touring the subcontinent for an Australian journalist is that by mid-afternoon on non-match days, deadlines back home have passed and you can spend a few hours wandering the streets. Cricket all day every day can send you stir-crazy. When you're in countries like Pakistan, India or Sri Lanka you cannot afford to waste a chance to get out there and immerse yourself in the place.

During the hearings in Lahore early in the 1998 tour, I found a brilliant guide. Shahid Hussain was a driver at the team hotel and we hit it off immediately. I would book him the day before for my morning trips to the court and for anything else in the afternoons. Shahid was small, wiry and fit. He did everything at full pace, as if life had not given him enough outlets for his energy and intelligence. He walked with a limp, the result of a street incident in which he'd been shot in the hip by thieves. The injury ended a promising international career in judo. He was determined to forge on regardless.

In the afternoons, Shahid would take me around the city. The first time, I said I wanted to photograph cricket being played in the streets and parks. No problem. He took me straight to a large park in the city centre where hundreds of people were playing tape-ball games with the light wooden bats that you can buy for a few rupees at shops all over the subcontinent. They are perfect for the backyard and beach cricket we play in Australia. The balls are tennis or rubber balls wrapped in masking tape to add weight and reduce bounce. Despite the history of great spin bowling in Pakistan, you don't see boys or young men delivering leg-breaks and wrong'uns on the maidans. Everyone bowls fast and full like Waqar Younis. As in Sri Lanka and India, most players in Pakistan display naturally correct technique and substantial skill.

Shahid's next stop was the huge pink Badshahi Mosque, built by the Moghuls in the seventeenth century. On an area of patchy grass on one side of the mosque, families sat around nibbling snacks and chatting while, nearby, young men lay sleeping in the afternoon sun. 'Drug addicts, sir,' Shahid said. 'What drugs, Shahid?' 'Heroin, sir. Smokin' heroin.' Around a corner I saw a game being played on the narrow pathway that hugs the high wall of the mosque; boys, teenagers and middle-aged men playing together as they do everywhere in Pakistan. They asked the question you hear everywhere on the subcontinent. 'Which country, sir?' The answer 'Australia' always brings approval. 'Ah, Australia very nice country, sir. Australia is best Test team in the world. Very good team, sir. Steve Wog, Mark Wog, Shen Warne. But Pakistan is best one-day team. Inzamam, sir. You must bat, sir, please.' Back at the hotel, Shahid asked if I was satisfied. 'Excellent, Shahid. Just what I wanted.' 'I know, sir. I know what you want. Shahid very smart, sir. Shahid genius.'

The High Court hearings meant that most of the press missed the official team visit to the Khyber Pass so a colleague and I decided to make use of Australia's early exit from the mini-World Cup in neighbouring Bangladesh to return to Peshawar. We took a car from Islamabad, drove over the beautiful Murree Hills and down across the plain to Peshawar, surviving the mandatory car accident on the final stretch. Two days later, we signed the forms, paid our fee, picked up the compulsory driver and armed guard from the Afridi tribe that rules the Khyber area and set off for the Pass, sixty kilometres to the west. As you leave the edges of the city, passing the jumble of the Smugglers' Bazaar, you go through a checkpoint before entering tribal territory. The area is still officially Pakistan but the government leaves the running of the area to the Pashtuns, whose main source of income is drug- and gun-running. In a barren, beautiful rocky landscape that resembled the moon more than the earth, we passed what looked like a dry riverbed. In the middle was a half-length pitch made of orange sand with a set of stumps at one end made of a Stonehenge-like pile of rocks.

Although the Murree Hills is not the only green, mountainous area in the country, my memories of Pakistan are of its flat, dry maidans, the fine dust that settles on everything during a day in Peshawar, the soft golden dusks that fall so quickly after a day's play and, of course, the exotic sound of the muezzin calling the faithful to prayer.

Tape-ball match — Lahore, October 1998

Evening prayers — cricket academy, National Stadium, Karachi, October 1998

Sports shop — Old City, Peshawar, October 1998

Pitch and stumps – near the Khyber Pass, North-West Frontier Province, November 1998

Colin Miller at a tour match — Karachi, September 1998

Uncle Cricket leading the chant 'Pakistan Zindabad' – second Test, Peshawar, October 1998

Police on the pavilion roof – second Test, Peshawar, October 1998

Boy outside a mosque — Lahore, October 1998

Outside the Badshahi Mosque — Lahore, October 1998

Saeed Anwar after play — second Test, Peshawar, October 1998

Spectators on a nearby roof — second Test, Peshawar, October 1998

Roadside game – Murree Hills, November 1998

Ticket window – third Test, Karachi, October 1998

Ricky Ponting (left) and Justin Langer after the third Test — Karachi, October 1998

Former Test off spinner Tauseef Ahmed – cricket academy, National Stadium, Karachi, October 1998

Khalid Mahmood, then president of the Pakistan Cricket Board – International Cricket Council meeting, Christchurch, New Zealand, January 1999

Alleged bookmaker Zafar Ali Jo-Jo waiting to give evidence to the Qayyum Inquiry into match-fixing – High Court, Lahore, October 1998

Match-fixer Salim Malik (second from left) during the match presentation after the second Test — Peshawar, October 1998